BEASTS by the BUNCHES

BEASTS by the BUNCHES

by A. Mifflin Lowe
illustrated by Susan J. Harrison

Doubleday & Company, Inc.
Garden City, New York

Library of Congress Cataloging-in-Publication Data

Lowe, A. Mifflin.
  Beasts by the bunches.

  Summary: An illustrated collection of poems about the strange-but-true names of various groups of animals, e.g. gaggle of geese, labor of moles, and sloth of bears.
  1. Animals—Juvenile poetry. 2. Zoology—Nomenclature (Popular)—Juvenile poetry. 3. Children's poetry, American. [1. English language—Terms and phrases—Poetry. 2. Animals—Poetry.
3. Zoology—Nomenclature (Popular)—Poetry. 4. American poetry]
I. Harrison, Susan, ill. II. Title.
PS3562.08814B4 1987   811'.54   86-24332
ISBN 0-385-23794-4
ISBN 0-385-23795-2 (lib. bdg.)

Art Direction by Diana Klemin
All Rights Reserved
Printed in Italy
First Edition

To Lexi and Colleen
A.M.L.

BEASTS BY THE BUNCHES

There are words you should know for each bunch of
    beasts
from the mightiest animals down to the least.
Now leopards, for instance, should be called a leap
and never a clowder, a clump or a creep.

And never say elephants live in a school,
for schools are all fish and you'll sound like a fool.
And don't you call lions a host or a herd
for pride is the only appropriate word.

Yes, there are words you should know for each bunch
    of beasts
from the mightiest animals down to the least.
So don't just go calling them all wild game,
for each group of animals has its own name.

A SLOTH OF BEARS

Why does a sloth of bears wear pajamas?
Is it merely to please their Papas and Mamas,
or just to keep warm in their cold, drafty lairs,
or is it so no one can call them bare bears?

A DRIFT OF HOGS

One day a drift of hungry hogs went slowly floating by,
their boat was made of marzipan with cheese and apple
  pie.
Their mast was formed of sausages, the sails were made
  of toast,
the cabin was a carrot cake, the rudder was a roast.
Their quandary was they couldn't eat, for if they ate
  they'd sink,
and all would fall into a sea from which they couldn't
  drink.
And even worse this sea, you see, was such a salty
  brine
'twould quickly pickle the wiggling feet of any
  swimming swine!
But at last, they got so famished that a large,
  emboldened sow
ate the mast and rudder and then started on the prow.
"Oh, no!" the others shouted out, "we dare not eat the
  boat
For even though we're all a drift, without it we can't
  float!"

A KNOT OF TOADS

Up and down the country roads
came hippity hopping a knot of toads.
Until at last they reached a fork
and ran into a large, white stork.
"Who are you?" the big bird cried.
"A knot of toads," the knot replied.
"A not?" the stork said scratching his head.
"No, a knot!" the toadies said.
"A 'not' like nothing?" said the bird.
"No, not that not—a different word!"
"A not like 'no'?" the stork asked then.
"No, not at all!" the toads chimed in.
"It's spelled with the "n" behind a "k,"
now step aside—you're in the way!"
"Not on your life," the big bird chirped
and ate them up (and later burped).
And up and down the country roads,
there now was not a knot of toads.

12

A SMACK OF JELLYFISH

Whacking and smacking and slapping along,
it's the jellyfish singing the jellyfish song.
Saying "Whoops, oops, pardon, oh please excuse me,"
they bump into each other all over the sea.
For having no feet to inhibit their motion,
they're carried about by the waves of the ocean.
And they make quite a jam when they get all that jelly
bunched up back to back and belly to belly.
So if down by the seaside you hear a loud squish,
it's surely a smack of some fat jellyfish.

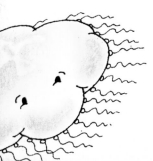

AN EXALTATION OF LARKS

Like small, feathered angels,
these beautiful birds
sing sweet hallelujahs
without using words.
For they've soared up so high
that they've captured the sound
of heaven and brought it back down to the ground.
And it fills human hearts with both joy and elation
to hear the larks singing in grand exaltation.

A LABOR OF MOLES

They work so hard although they're blind
in shallow holes that twist and wind.
They dig from dusk until the dawn
and push up lumps all through your lawn.
But just a footstep on the ground
can make their tunnels tumble down.
So once again these sons of toil
begin to work beneath the soil.
Yes, it's true that moles don't have much fun,
for a labor's labor's never done.

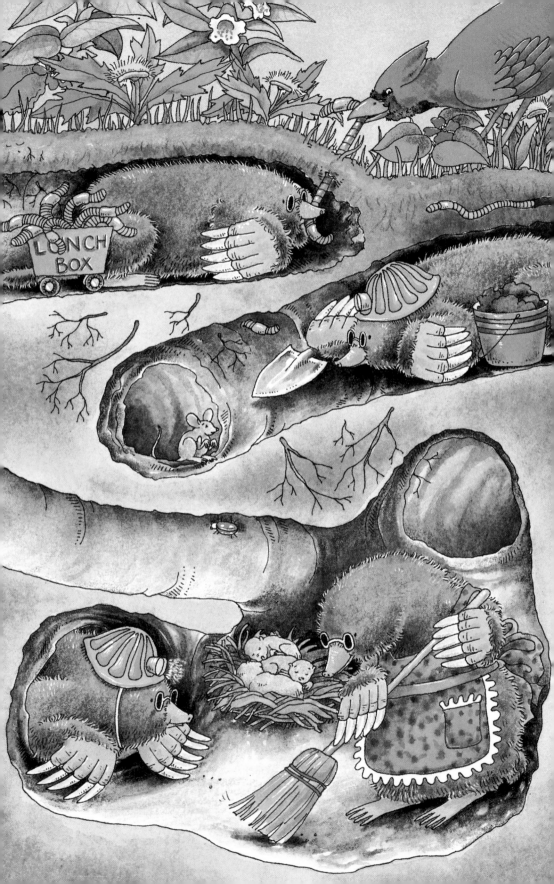

A GAGGLE OF GEESE

"Oh who could have strangled the gaggle of geese?"
Said the duck as he picked up a small piece of fleece.
"Why the horsies of course," said the pigs with a fuss.
"No, no," said the horses, "it sure wasn't us.
For we used to love how the gaggle would wiggle
and even the way they would snicker and giggle."
"Well perhaps," said the duck, "it was done by the
    sheep."
"Oh no," the sheep baa-ed as they started to weep,
"for we used to love how they'd waddle around,
and make little marks with their feet in the ground."
"Well somebody here had the gaggle's goose cooked,"
said the duck as he gave them a hard piercing look.
"But why would we do it?" asked the goat with a
    bleat.
"For none of us animals even eats meat."
But off in the corner the farmer's small niece
smiled as she thought of the gaggle of geese,
and how good they would look and how good they
    would smell,
and how good they would taste when the geese were
    cooked well.

A SHREWDNESS OF APES

If a shrewdness of apes is so clever,
why do they live where they do?
Why don't they live in a nice house somewhere
in a city or suburb like me and like you?
Oh why must they dwell where it's sticky and hot
without all the wonderful stuff that we've got?!
But consider the issue from their point of view
and you just might wish you were one of them, too.
Yes, apes may be smarter than you might suppose
for out in the jungle they never need clothes,
(tight-fitting girdles and toe-pinching shoes
are items of clothing they just never use);
and the wealthiest ape has no more than the poor
so they don't need a padlock or even a door;
(no, there's nothing to lose or to make or to lend,
since money is something that apes never spend),
and, having no army, they can't have a war,
but anyway, what would they be fighting for,
since all they must do is eat, sleep, and drink,
and occasionally gaze at the sky while they think?
Yes, maybe a shrewdness of apes is so smart
that they just choose to stay where they are
and we aren't.

A TROOP OF KANGAROOS

It's not a troop of brownies,
it's not a troop of men,
it's not a troop of actors
that's marching through the glen.
With their fuzzy tails and pouches
and their voices like kazoos,
there's nothing else it could be
but a troop of kangaroos.

A PARLIAMENT OF OWLS

Once a parliament of owls
with long, gray beards and sagging jowls
sat talking of the local rabbits,
recounting all their nasty habits.

While shaking his great, hoary head
the oldest of the owls said,
"Something simply must be done,
they're always having too much fun,
and there really ought to be some laws
against the way they lick their paws."

26

"Oh yes," the others all agreed,
"rabbits are a filthy breed.
All they do is sit and munch
on dirty carrots by the bunch.
They smell as bad as rotten cheese
and worst of all they carry fleas."

But when some rabbits scampered by,
the owls smiled and all said, "Hi,"
and asked them all about their day
and wished them well along the way.

But when they'd gone, the oldest owl
sat there with a fearsome scowl.
"Rabbits," he said, "they make me sick.
I'd like to give them all a kick."

"Oh yes," the others all agreed,
"they're just a dirty, filthy breed."

A PRIDE OF LIONS

In zoos they're just pathetic beasts
not regal, vain, or proud.
And the noise they make is more of a moan
than a roar that's fierce and loud.
And some just eat and yawn and stretch,
becoming fat and lazy.
While others pace about the cage
until they're almost crazy.
And it's hard to think when you watch them sit
and eat their T-bone feasts,
that the mangy cats you're looking at
could be the Kings of Beasts.
But in the jungles where they live it's quite a different
    story.
Their teeth are fierce, their manes are long, their claws
    are often gory,
and their roars are such a giant sound they shake the
    night apart
and make you tremble in your bed with terror in your
    heart.
Then all the other jungle beasts just slink away and
    hide.
And you wouldn't ask if you saw them there why a
    family's called a pride.

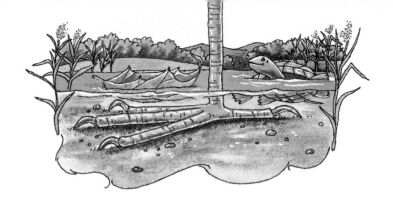

A SIEGE OF HERONS

If you've ever seen them standing
on a single, skinny leg,
or sitting neatly on a nest
to try and hatch an egg,
you just might be inclined to think
that "siege" was not the name
for a bunch of birds that seem to be
so fragile, weak, and tame.
But when a minnow sees a siege
of herons that comes stalking,
it looks to him like giant beasts
are in the water walking.
And so you see how something looks
is largely up to you.
It can look big and tall or very small
depending on your point of view.

A POD OF WHALES

A pod of whales was swimming all through a peaceful
  sea
and what a whale of a sight it was for a small fry such
  as me!
They leaped and rolled and splashed about like puppies
  left to play.
They slapped their tails and spouted out great plumes
  of spumy spray.
But when the sea grew wild, whipped high by wicked
  gales,
they knew that they must calm it down with songs
  known just to whales.
So they held their breath for a day or two and dived
  into the gloom,
and there they sang sad, magic songs in a deep,
  bassoony boom.
They sang of looming icebergs, they sang of gliding
  sharks,
they sang of merry mermen and of sunken, Spanish
  barques.

They sang of foam and fairy tales and everything that
    floats,
they sang of sails and ivory and men in wooden boats.
They sang of pirate treasure ships all laden down with
    gold,
they sang of all the colors that a coral reef can hold.
They sang of silver bubbles spinning slowly overhead,
they sang a chantey sung by men when lost and left for
    dead.
They sang of soaring flying fish that arc against the
    sky,
they sang in tranquil tender tones and only paused to
    sigh.
Then when their songs were all sung out they fell into
    a trance
and ended all their singing with a slow and doleful
    dance.
Then up they shot like comets from the bottom of the
    sea,
and in the silence left behind, now all was harmony.
Yes, in the silence left behind, now all was harmony.

33

A CRASH OF RHINOCEROI

Now a rhino's eyesight is downright stinky
(which makes his whole world look all murky and
    inky)
so although they can run very quickly and well,
just which way they're headed they can't always tell.
And thus when they meet with the rest of the gang,
they're known as a crash (with a boom and a bang).

A MURDER OF CROWS

They're dressed all in black from their heads to their
    toes,
so you'd better look out, it's a murder of crows.
They'll step on your shoes and throw sand in your
    eyes.
They'll answer your questions with nothing but lies.
They're mean and they're rotten and vicious and snide.
It's a murder of crows, so you'd better go hide.

A MISSION OF MONKEYS

Oh, mission of monkeys, now what have you done
in your unceasing efforts to always have fun?
There's no place to swing 'cause you've pulled all the
    vines
out of the trees with your dumb monkeyshines.
You've bent every monkey bar from which you have
    hung
and snapped every springboard from which you have
    sprung.
(Oh, mission of monkeys, you're such silly boys
that you've gone and destroyed all your favorite toys!)
And even when dressed in your best monkey suits,
you keep on behaving like rude, little brutes.
And each time you leave someone's house in a wreck,
you just walk away saying, "Awwwww, what the heck!"
(Yes, you've gone through this life as though no one
    else matters
and left every place all in pieces and tatters!)
So if you should wonder why folks look affrighted
when you come unannounced and, of course, uninvited,
it's just that they can't guess what damage you'll do
in your endless amusement at you being you.

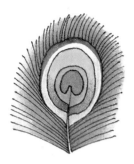

A MUSTER OF PEACOCKS

Now what would you call some peacocks all standing in
    a group?
A glory or a strut perhaps, a swagger or a swoop?
A grandeur or a splendor or a finery or pomp?
A posture or a posing, a regalia or a romp?
Yes, you'd think that being beautiful they'd have a
    lovely name.
But the truth of this sad matter (and it really is a
    shame),
is that the name we've given them completely lacks in
    luster,
for when they stand together they're called nothing but
    a muster.

A RAG OF COLTS

One curious day a rag of colts
galloped out of the barn like lightning bolts,
and running without either riders or reins,
they went through the valley like uncontrolled trains.
First they flashed through the forest and splashed
    through a stream,
then they ran through the village and made people
    scream.
Next they went to the farmlands and trampled
    tomatoes,
stomped on the stringbeans and mashed the potatoes.
Then they pranced in a circle and they danced up and
    down,
like the gay painted ponies in a merry-go-round.
Oh, they're impossible to stop when they're feeling
    their oats,
'cause there's nothing quite as crazy as a wild rag of
    colts!

A LEAP OF LEOPARDS

Look!
It's a leap of leopards that's jumping so high,
they look like they're almost a part of the sky.
A leap of leopards that's jumping so fast
before you can see them they're already past.
A leap of leopards as light as the breeze
and yellow as butter, bananas, or bees.
Oh, why don't they stop all this leaping around
and just try to keep their feet on the ground?

Yes, it's a leap of leopards that's jumping so far
on their very next leap they might land on a star.
A leap of leopards that seems without care,
they're soaring so blissfully into the air.
Oh, why don't they stop all this leaping around
and just try to keep their feet on the ground?

A WATCH OF NIGHTINGALES

They're sitting in your window,
they're perched in every tree.
Nightingales are watching you when you go to sleep.
They'll stroke your eyes with velvet wings,
they'll sing you songs and bring your dreams.
Nightingales are watching you when you go to sleep.
And if you have an evil dream
that makes you want to cry and scream,
the nightingales will fly away
and turn the nighttime into day.
So you can close your heavy eyes
and I can say, "Sleep tight."
A watch of nightingales is going
to watch you through the night.

DATE DUE			
NOV 0 9 2004			
NOV 1 6 2004			